GARDENING TASKS THROUGH THE YEAR

A practical guide to year-round success in your
garden, shown in over 125 photographs

ANDREW MIKOLAJSKI

LORENZ BOOKS

This edition is published by Lorenz Books
an imprint of Anness Publishing Ltd
Blaby Road, Wigston, Leicestershire LE18 4SE
info@anness.com

www.lorenzbooks.com; www.annesspublishing.com

If you like the images in this book and would like to investigate using
them for publishing, promotions or advertising, please visit our website
www.practicalpictures.com for more information.

© Anness Publishing Ltd 2013

A CIP catalogue record for this book
is available from the British Library.

Publisher: Joanna Lorenz
Editor: Valerie Ferguson
Photography: Peter Anderson, Jonathan Buckley, John Freeman,
Michelle Garrett, Andrea Jones and Simon McBride
Series Designer: Larraine Shamwana
Designer: Andrew Heath
Production Controller: Ben Worley

PUBLISHER'S NOTE
Although the advice and information in this book are believed to be accurate and
true at the time of going to press, neither the authors nor the publisher can
accept any legal responsibility or liability for any errors or omissions that may
have been made nor for any inaccuracies nor for any loss, harm or injury that
comes about from following instructions or advice in this book.

CONTENTS

Introduction

KEEPING A GARDEN LOOKING GOOD ALL YEAR ROUND SHOULD NEVER BECOME A BURDEN. SPREADING ESSENTIAL TASKS THROUGHOUT THE SEASONS, SO THAT THE GARDEN IS ALWAYS UNDER CONTROL, WILL ENSURE THAT IT REMAINS A PLEASURE EVEN AT THE BUSIEST TIMES.

Gardening has never been so popular, and it is quite easy to see why. With increasing urbanization and the proliferation of new technologies, most of us seem to spend large parts of our lives either commuting to and from work or sitting in front of computer screens. It is small wonder that the idea of getting back to nature and growing things in a hands-on way is so appealing, even if all we have is a small suburban garden or just a tiny backyard with a few containers.

FORWARD PLANNING

Good gardeners are always thinking about the future, and forward planning is important if the garden is always to look its best. However, with the busy lives that most of us lead these days, it is easy to overlook some of the simple gardening tasks that will save time in the long run – hence the value of a mini season-by-season guide to gardening activities.

No gardening calendar can ever be followed rigidly, of course, because

Above: Successional sowing of vegetables in spring will ensure that your kitchen garden plots are well filled and productive all summer long.

4

not only does the climate vary from one part of the country to another, but the weather is never the same two years running. In one year a bumper crop of slugs will wreak havoc on your young plants, but in another you may hardly be troubled by them. Fruit crops may be delayed to early or mid-autumn by late spring frosts or may be ready for harvesting in late summer. Nevertheless, even given the vagaries of the weather, it is possible to list the main tasks in the general order in which they should be done so that you can complete them when you have time and when the weather permits you to get into the garden to carry them out.

Above: Give a summer hanging basket a head-start by planting it in spring and keeping it in a greenhouse until there is no more fear of late frosts.

WORKING WITH THE SEASONS

Fortunately, many plants are forgiving and allow you a certain amount of leeway if certain tasks are mis-timed. A mild, damp winter, for example, might mean that your roses burst into growth, persuading you that they need pruning early. If a sudden cold spell kills off the resulting new growth, you can simply prune them again and reconcile yourself to the fact that flowering may be a bit later than usual. The plants don't seem to mind.

It's a good idea to make staggered sowings of vegetables or summer bedding plants, so that you always have reserve stock should any early sowings fail. If you do not have a greenhouse, you can make use of your kitchen windowsill to start seeds into growth several weeks earlier than if you wait to sow them outdoors.

HOW TO USE THIS BOOK

This book is organized by season, with each season further subdivided into early, mid and late to coincide broadly with the months of the year. Within each mini-season, tasks for the ornamental garden, kitchen garden and greenhouse or conservatory are described, with handy, at-a-glance checklists of the main jobs to be done. The more important tasks are dealt with in greater depth, with pictures showing the correct techniques. A glossary explains the few technical terms that are used here and there.

Early Spring

THE BEGINNING OF THE NATURAL YEAR IS AN EXCITING TIME IN THE
GARDEN, EVEN IF WINTER CANNOT YET BE ENTIRELY FORGOTTEN.
MANY PLANTS ARE BEGINNING TO WAKE UP FROM THEIR WINTER
DORMANCY AND TO PUT OUT FRESH GREEN SHOOTS.

THE ORNAMENTAL GARDEN

Despite the cold, early spring is a good
time to make a start on many outdoor
jobs. The soil is starting to warm up
and spring rains will help plants estab-
lish well and get off to a good start.

Planting

As long as the soil is not waterlogged
or frozen, early spring is one of the
best times to plant new shrubs and

Above: A welcome sight in early spring,
Muscari armeniacum *'Blue Spike' forms
clumps that can be divided in summer.*

perennials. Prepare the ground first,
digging over the whole area thoroughly
and removing any perennial weeds,
such as couch grass and bindweed.
Fork in plenty of well-rotted garden
compost or farmyard manure and add
a handful of a slow-release granular
fertilizer or some bonemeal. Dig a
hole twice the width of the plant's
container, slide the plant out of the
pot, carefully tease out its roots and
set it in the centre of the hole. Backfill
with the excavated soil, firming it in
well, and water thoroughly.

Sowing Hardy Annuals

Hardy annual seeds, such as hawks-
beard (*Crepis rubra*), poached-egg
plant (*Limnanthes douglasii*) and
love-in-a-mist (*Nigella damsascena*),
can be sown where the plants are to
flower. Weed the ground and rake it
level, then sow the seeds in rows
(which makes weeding easier) or by
sprinkling (broadcasting) it over the
ground. Cover the seed lightly and
water in dry weather. When the
seedlings are large enough to handle,
thin them to the distances recommended on the seed packets.

LAYING TURF

Early spring is a good time to make a new lawn, either by sowing grass seed or by laying turf. Although turf is the more expensive option, it does provide an instant result. However, after a few years you will not be able to tell the difference between a seed-raised lawn and bought-in turfs.

2 Lay a plank on top of the row of turf you have just laid, and use this to spread your weight when laying the second and subsequent rows, moving it as necessary. Butt the second row of turfs tight against the first, but stagger any joints between the strips like the bonds in brickwork.

1 Start by marking out the area of the new lawn. Dig over the area, removing any large stones, and take out all traces of perennial weeds. Taking very small steps, tread over the area to consolidate the soil, then rake the surface level. Lay the first strip of turf along a straight edge.

3 Tamp down each row of turf using the back of a rake. Trim the edges, if necessary, after the turf is laid, using a half-moon edger. In dry weather, water the new lawn frequently until it is established.

GARDENER'S TIP
Keep all new plantings well watered until they are established.

7

THE KITCHEN GARDEN

Now is your best opportunity to improve the soil in the kitchen garden, which can become impoverished over time. To improve its structure and moisture-retentiveness, dig in plenty of organic matter such as well-rotted farmyard manure or garden compost. A general fertilizer such as bonemeal, or a granular fertilizer, will break down gradually as the crops grow. Use organic or chemical formulations as you wish, but follow the quantities recommended by the manufacturer.

Above: Space onion sets about 15cm (6in) apart and cover with soil, leaving just the tips of the bulbs protruding.

This is also a good time to plant onion sets in a shallow drill, made with the corner of a hoe or rake. If birds disturb the sets, simply push them back into the ground.

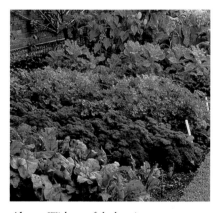

Above: With careful planning, even a small border can accommodate both ornamental plants and vegetables.

Keeping Seedlings Warm

Sowing seed can be a gamble, because a sudden cold snap can cause vulnerable seedlings to rot or run to seed, but if you cannot wait to get busy, cover the seeds with horticultural fleece, which is a virtually foolproof way of ensuring a good crop. It will warm up the soil as well as providing protection from frost and pests. It allows light and moisture through to keep plants growing but will not squash them.

Perforated plastic film is an alternative to fleece. A cloche – a sheet of film stretched over wire supports – can be used to protect larger seedlings.

**THINGS TO DO
IN THE KITCHEN GARDEN**
Apply fertilizers
Warm up the soil with cloches or fleece
Plant new strawberries
Chit seed potatoes
Plant onion sets or shallots
Sow vegetable seeds (in mild areas only)

THE GREENHOUSE

You can steal a march on other gardeners by raising new plants from seed under glass before the weather has really warmed up. Even if your greenhouse is not heated, the extra shelter will make it possible for you to sow the seed of half-hardy annuals and tender vegetables, which can be potted up as they germinate. Don't forget, however, that a bright windowsill can be just as useful.

USING A PROPAGATOR

You can speed up the germination of early sowings using a propagator. A heated propagator will give you even more options, especially if it is thermostatically controlled.

1 Use different containers for different seeds. Square or oblong seed trays that fit snugly into the propagator make the most economical use of the space. The modules on the right are useful for small seedlings, such as ageratums, or for seeds that are large enough to sow individually.

> ### THINGS TO DO
> ### IN THE GREENHOUSE
> Start begonias and gloxinias into growth
> Pot on cuttings of pelargoniums
> and fuchsias
> Prick out tender seedlings
> Ventilate the greenhouse on warm days

2 An unheated propagator should be placed in a warm position in the greenhouse. Adjust the ventilation as soon as the seeds have germinated.

Keeping Hippeastrums

If you have grown hippeastrum bulbs for winter flowers, instead of discarding the bulbs when the flowers are over, you can try building them up for flowering next year.

Keep the plants growing in a warm, bright spot and feed and water them regularly as long as the leaves are growing strongly. Stop watering as the leaves start to turn yellow and die back, and store the bulbs in dry potting mix until the winter. Flowering cannot be guaranteed, but it is worth the attempt.

Starting off Begonias

Tuberous begonias can be started into growth now. Set the tubers on the surface of the potting mix, in either individual pots or trays. Look for emerging shoots or place the concave surface of each tuber uppermost. Keep them in a warm, light place and water as the shoots develop.

Mid-spring

THE GARDEN WILL BEGIN TO FILL WITH COLOUR AS THE WEATHER WARMS UP AND THE DAYS LENGTHEN. MID-SPRING IS THE BEST TIME FOR MOVING AND DIVIDING PLANTS AND FOR SOWING SEEDS IN READINESS FOR THE JOYS OF SUMMER DISPLAYS TO COME.

THE ORNAMENTAL GARDEN

As the sap rises with the warmer weather, work in the garden can begin in earnest. This is a great time for pruning shrubs, either to revive neglected specimens or to keep vigorous species within bounds. You also need to plan for the big events of summer in the herbaceous border by setting stakes and ties in position.

Pruning Bush Roses

The old, rather rigorous rules for rose pruning have been reappraised and relaxed in recent years, but some long-

Above: This old rose needs little more than a general tidy up. Old wood should be cut out completely.

established principles remain. Cut out any damaged and diseased wood completely, then assess the rest of the bush. Spindly shoots are unlikely to bear flowers, so cut them back hard to stimulate stronger growth. Shoots that are already growing strongly need cutting back only lightly, if at all. If the centre of the bush is overcrowded, with lots of crossing branches, thin these out. Feed the rose with a special rose fertilizer and water it in, then apply a generous mulch of well-rotted organic matter.

Supporting Summer Climbers

Climbing plants, such as sweet peas (*Lathyrus odoratus*), look sensational rising above smaller plants in summer borders. Although you can buy ready-made obelisks and tripods, it is easy to make your own using bamboo canes,

---

**THINGS TO DO
IN THE ORNAMENTAL GARDEN**
Plant aquatic plants
Sow sweet peas and other annuals
Stake border plants
Take softwood cuttings
Prune early-flowering shrubs
Trim winter-flowering heathers

Above: Make a support for sweet peas by driving bamboo canes into the soil in a circle. Bind at the top with wire or string.

Above: Plants with large, heavy flowers, such as Paeonia lactiflora 'Bowl of Beauty', will benefit from staking.

held together at the top with garden twine. You can also buy special plastic grips, which are designed to hold the canes securely at the top. Put one plant at the base of each cane.

Staking Plants

Some border plants that have large, heavy flowers, such as peonies and delphiniums, need staking if the weight of the flower is not to bring the stem crashing down. Stakes should be set in position before the stems grow too tall, so that new growth can be fastened to the supports as it develops.

There are a number of ways of supporting plants, depending on their habit. In an informal, cottage garden border, twigs can be pushed into the ground around the plants; they will soon be hidden by the leafy growth.

Bamboo canes are best for tall, single-stemmed plants like delphiniums, but shorter, clump-forming plants, such as some peonies, can be effectively supported with a ring stake, which can be raised as the stems grow.

Above: Set up proprietary supports early in the season, so that herbaceous plants can grow up through the framework.

11

THE KITCHEN GARDEN

Although the weather is still unpredictable, the soil should be warming up sufficiently for you to consider planting out seedlings of cabbages, broccoli and cauliflower when they have been hardened off. You should also make further sowings of onion sets and shallots to give a longer cropping season.

Remember, however, that late frosts can kill tender young shoots, so be prepared to cover vulnerable plants with horticultural fleece, cloches or even sheets of newspaper if frosty weather is forecast.

Protecting Blossom

A spell of warm spring weather will encourage fruit trees to produce blossom, but an air frost at this time can do untold harm. This occurs when the temperature of the air about 1.2m (4ft) above ground level falls below freezing point at night, freezing the moisture in the blossom and in other tender shoots. When the temperature rises in the morning, the cell walls of the plant tissue often burst, damaging the blossom so that it never sets fruit. Pears are particularly badly affected by this problem, as they tend to flower early.

**THINGS TO DO
IN THE VEGETABLE GARDEN**
Sow maincrop vegetables
Plant potatoes
Transplant cabbages and cauliflowers
Apply a mulch of well-rotted compost
to fruit bushes
Protect early strawberries
Protect blossom on fruit trees

Above: *Sowing vegetables in rows makes subsequent weeding of the plot easier, as it allows annual weeds to be quickly removed with a hoe.*

Wall-trained fruit trees can be protected most easily by draping sheets of plastic or even fine netting over a framework. Free-standing standard trees are more difficult to protect, although horticultural fleece can be used. If you use plastic sheeting, make sure it is held above the plant and cannot touch the young shoots, which might otherwise rot. Remove the protection during the day so that insects can pollinate the blossom.

PLANTING POTATOES

You will get the best results if you chit the potatoes before planting. Chitted potatoes get off to a quicker start than unchitted tubers, and this is a useful method of staggering crops. Chitted tubers are those that have begun to sprout, and to encourage this you should place the tubers in a light, frost-free position – a windowsill indoors is ideal.

Potatoes can be planted through a heavy-duty black plastic sheet, which saves the trouble of having to earth (hill) them up. Cultivate the soil, then cover the area with the sheet, holding it down around the edges with soil. Cut X-shaped slits in the sheet at regular intervals and plant the tubers through these.

If you prefer to plant your potatoes in the traditional way, cover the soil with a cloche for a week or two before planting to warm it up.

1 Use a draw hoe or a spade to make flat-bottomed drills 10–13cm (4–5in) deep and 50–75cm (20–30in) apart in prepared soil.

2 Space the tubers 30–45cm (12–18in) apart along each drill, making sure that the buds (eyes) or shoots face upward.

3 Pull over the excavated soil to cover the tubers or cover them with a sheet of heavy-duty black plastic, held down in the soil.

GARDENER'S TIP
If you want larger potatoes, once you have chitted the tubers rub off all but three of the shoots before planting.

13

Midspring

THE GREENHOUSE
This is the time of year when most gardeners wish they had a larger greenhouse. Not only are all the seedlings from earlier sowings now ready to be pricked out or potted up, but tender vegetables, including outdoor tomatoes and runner beans, can be sown under glass now.

PLANTING A HANGING BASKET
Hanging baskets are associated with high summer and are planted up in late spring, usually at the time when it is safe to put tender plants outdoors. However, if you have a greenhouse or conservatory that provides protection from frost, or, better still, one that is heated, you can get your baskets off to a flying start now and have a mature display earlier in the season.

Above: The trailing habit of the tender fuchsia 'Dark Eyes' makes it an ideal subject for a hanging basket.

1 Rest the basket in a bucket or large pot to keep it steady and line it with moss or a hanging basket liner. Half-fill with a suitable potting mix.

2 Set trailing plants around the sides of the basket, laying them on their sides. Add more compost to cover the rootballs.

3 Place larger plants in the centre, fill any gaps with potting mix and water well. Hang the basket in a light, sheltered place.

GARDENER'S TIP
Use water-retaining crystals in hanging baskets to reduce the likelihood of the contents drying out in summer.

14

Sowing Tender Vegetables

For early crops of tender vegetables, such as marrows, courgettes (zucchini) and outdoor cucumbers, sow now in small pots, filled with seed potting mix to within about 2.5cm (1in) of the rim. Water the potting mix and allow it to drain before sowing the seed, which should be lightly covered with sieved potting mix. Keep in a warm, light place until the seeds germinate, then grow them on under cover until

Above: Courgette (zucchini) plants germinated in the greenhouse need to be hardened off in a cold frame before they can be planted outside.

all risk of frost has passed. Transfer them to a cold frame to acclimatize before planting them out in their final positions in the garden.

Above: Sow two or three seeds of outdoor cucumbers in each pot, setting them on edge, and lightly cover with potting mix.

THINGS TO DO
IN THE GREENHOUSE
Sow tender vegetables
Prick out or pot up seedlings
Take leaf cuttings of flowering
houseplants, such as *Saintpaulia*
and *Streptocarpus*
Decrease the water given to cyclamen
Take cuttings of tender perennials
Check for vine weevil grubs when
repotting plants

15

Late Spring

THIS IS MANY PEOPLE'S FAVOURITE SEASON IN THE GARDEN, WHEN
PLANTS ARE GROWING STRONGLY BUT WITH ALL THE FRESHNESS OF
YOUTH STILL UPON THEM. YOU SHOULD STILL BE ALERT FOR LATE
FROSTS AND GIVE ANY FROST-PRONE PLANTS ADEQUATE PROTECTION.

THE ORNAMENTAL GARDEN

Unseasonal weather, in the form of
late frosts or extremely wet or windy
weather, can still cause problems, so
keep an eye on forecasts and be ready
to protect vulnerable plants. After
especially strong winds, check that all
newly planted shrubs and perennials
are still firmly bedded into the soil and
have not been affected by wind rock.

Bedding Plants

Half-hardy annuals that you have
raised under glass can now be hardened off – that is, acclimatized to outdoor conditions. Place them outdoors
in a spot that is sheltered from strong

*Above: Many gardeners regard water
lilies, such as this* Nymphaea *'Attraction',
as the most desirable of all water plants.*

sun and wind for increasingly longer
periods during the day. Move them
back under cover at night, either
indoors or into a cold frame. They can
be planted out in their final positions
once all danger of frost has passed.

> ### THINGS TO DO
> ### IN THE ORNAMENTAL GARDEN
> Plant hanging baskets
> Harden off bedding plants
> Clip evergreen hedges
> Prune *Clematis montana* after
> flowering, if necessary
> Deadhead flowered bulbs

PLANTING A WATER LILY

If you have a garden pond, this is the most convenient time of year to plant water lilies, which should now be producing signs of fresh growth. Water lilies should be planted as soon as possible after purchase to ensure that the rhizomes do not dry out. Plant them in baskets specially designed for aquatic plants; those with a fine mesh do not need lining, but open-sided baskets should be lined with coarse hessian (burlap).

1 If necessary, line the aquatic planting basket and half-fill with garden soil or specially formulated potting mix. Place the water lily rhizome on top and cover with more soil, leaving the buds exposed.

2 Place a good layer of stones or gravel on the surface so that soil does not float out of the basket. Hold the basket under the surface of the pool to flood it with water, then gently lower it to the appropriate depth to allow the leaves to float on the surface, supporting it on bricks if necessary.

Above: If necessary, prune the vigorous Clematis montana *'Elizabeth' after it has finished flowering.*

Hedges

Evergreen hedges should be given their first trim about now. To make sure the top is level, run a string between two uprights as a guide. If you are using power tools (possibly on loan from a hire shop), make sure you follow any safety advice and remember to wear gloves, goggles and ear protectors.

Above: As well as clipping hedges, now is the time to neaten up topiary specimens, such as this spiral bay (Laurus nobilis).

THE KITCHEN GARDEN

When you are planting out in the kitchen garden, remember that successional sowing and planting will reduce gluts and give you a continuous supply of vegetables and fruit over a longer period.

Intercropping

One of the best ways of making good use of every available scrap of ground is to grow some quick-growing plants,

*Above: Mints, including the variegated applemint (*Mentha suaveolens *'Variegata'), are vigorous plants that can be divided now. Restricting the roots by growing them in containers, or a separate bed will stop them becoming too invasive.*

such as cut-and-come-again lettuces or radishes, in the spaces between larger, slower-growing plants, such as Brussels sprouts and parsnips. Not only will this give you two crops in the space of one, but it will also help to keep down weeds by covering what would otherwise be bare soil. Do not overcrowd plants, however, or they will compete with each other for available light, air and nutrients, and all the crops will suffer.

Although combining a variety of different plants in your vegetable plot can minimize the incidence of pests and diseases, there are some crops that should not be grown close together. Onions and garlic, for example, do not grow well alongside beans and peas, and potatoes should not be combined with cucumbers, marrows and courgettes (zucchini).

There are also some herbs that can be invasive. Mint is the most notorious, but you might also consider growing tansy *(Tanacetum vulgare)* and woodruff *(Asperula odorata* syn. *Galium odoratum)* in pots too.

THINGS TO DO
IN THE KITCHEN GARDEN
Sow sweetcorn (corn)
Sow rootcrops such as beetroot (beets),
carrots and parsnips
Plant outdoor tomatoes
Plant runner (green) and pole beans
Lift and divide mint
Hoe around vegetables to
keep weeds down

PLANTING RUNNER BEANS

Runner (green) beans are twining climbers that need support, and a wigwam of canes is the most economical use of space. In warm areas, simply plant a seed at the base of each cane. In cold districts, it is better to raise seedlings under cover and delay planting out until the threat of frosts has gone.

1 Crossing pairs of canes in rows is an alternative method of supporting beans and is useful if your plot is rectangular.

2 Plant one runner (green) bean plant at the base of each support and water in well. As the stems grow, twine them around the canes.

Growing Outdoor Tomatoes

Many gardeners find outdoor tomatoes an easier proposition than indoor ones, because they need less maintenance, although the crops will be smaller and the season is shorter. The plants must still be raised from seed under cover. If you don't want to sow seed, you can usually buy small plants for growing on from garden centres. Harden them off first, before planting them out in containers or growing bags. Wait until all risk of frost has passed before planting them out.

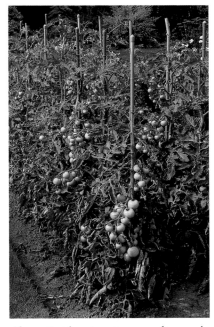

Above: Outdoor tomatoes are often much tastier than those grown under glass, particularly if the summer has been hot and the fruit is able to ripen well.

The Greenhouse

It is not too late to sow tomatoes, marrows, melons, ridge cucumbers, courgettes (zucchini), pumpkins, sweetcorn (corn) and half-hardy annuals.

On warm, sunny days make sure that the greenhouse is well ventilated. Humid, still air will encourage fungal diseases, and seedlings will die. A common problem in a poorly ventilated, overcrowded greenhouse is damping off, a disease that causes seedlings to collapse at soil level. Use sterile pots and new potting mix for seeds and do not overwater. If you do not mind using chemicals in the greenhouse, apply a fungicidal drench to the potting mix before sowing.

Above: Melons need a sturdy framework to support the growing plants. Nets slung above the containers hold the fruit.

Growing Indoor Tomatoes

Indoor tomatoes, either raised from seed or bought in as young plants, can now be planted. Because tomatoes cannot be grown in the same soil year after year, it is best to use growing bags or large containers. To support the growing plants (unless you are growing the bush or dwarf types), erect a cane next to each of the plants or train them on strings.

1 Cut holes in the growing bags according to the instructions printed on the side. Most growing bags will accommodate three plants, but make sure that when you plant the tomatoes they are the recommended distance apart.

2 Fix a horizontal wire across the greenhouse, as high above the plants as possible. Fix a second length of wire parallel to the first but near ground level. Tie a length of string between the two wires in line with each plant. Loop the string around the growing tip of each plant, so that it grows in a spiral shape.

Above: Control greenhouse pests by introducing natural predators such as parasitic wasps, effective against whitefly.

Biological Controls

The warm, humid atmosphere of a greenhouse is the perfect environment for insect pests, but increasing numbers of these can be controlled with other insects so that you do not have to use chemicals. The beneficial insects are released on to the susceptible plants in order to attack the pest.

Whitefly, spider mites, soft scale insects and thrips can be controlled by this method. Remember that once a biological control has been introduced, you should not use pesticides of any kind (or you will also kill the predators) and you should also remove any sticky traps that you put up earlier in the year.

Above: Bell peppers are increasingly popular as a greenhouse crop. They appreciate the extra heat and humidity that the enclosed environment provides.

21

Early Summer

EVERY TIME YOU STEP INTO THE GARDEN AT THIS TIME OF YEAR, YOU ARE GREETED BY A MASS OF FRESH NEW FOLIAGE AND FLOWERS. THE KITCHEN GARDEN IS COMING INTO ITS OWN NOW, PROVIDING A WONDERFUL FEAST OF HOME-GROWN PRODUCE FOR THE TABLE.

THE ORNAMENTAL GARDEN

Early summer is a transitional period in the flower garden, and there may be a week or two between the spring-flowering plants and bulbs dying down and the summer bedding coming into flower. Focus attention on the patio and create an instant display by planting up pots and troughs that will provide colour and interest now and for the rest of the summer.

PLANTING A CONTAINER

By now it is safe to leave tender plants outdoors, and because these are usually long-flowering, they make ideal subjects for a container planting.

2 Place a feature plant in the centre of the arrangement. An osteospermum, such as the one chosen here, will carry on flowering until well into the autumn.

3 Position other flowering plants and trailers around the osteospermum to soften the edge of the container, then fill the gaps with more potting mix. Water well to settle the plants.

1 Line the base of a large container with crocks and half-fill with potting mix.

Pruning Shrubs

Now is the time to tidy up any early-flowering shrubs, which will be putting on rapid growth. Remove all faded flowers, then cut back any damaged branches and remove the thick, old growth entirely, reaching into the base of the plant with loppers if necessary. Shorten the remaining stems to

Above: Inspect lilies, such as these Asiatic hybrids, for signs of the bright red lily beetle, a serious pest of lilies and fritillaries.

produce an open, well-balanced plant, cutting back thin shoots hard but trimming vigorous ones only lightly.

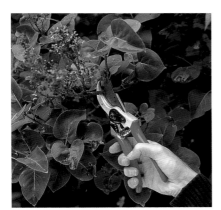

Above: As soon as lilacs finish flowering, deadhead them by cutting back to the first pair of leaves below the flowerhead.

THINGS TO DO
IN THE ORNAMENTAL GARDEN

Sow hardy annuals for late flowers
Move hanging baskets outdoors
Check lilies for signs of lily beetle
Plant containers for summer interest
Layer climbers to increase your stock
Prune early-flowering shrubs
Feed lawns
Deadhead rhododendrons

GARDENER'S TIP

Choose containers that are as large as possible. Not only will they dry out more slowly, but they will also provide the most impressive display. Move the container into position before filling it with potting mix and plants: it will be too heavy to move when it is full.

THE KITCHEN GARDEN

Keep an eye on newly planted-out seedlings so that you can take prompt action to prevent pests and diseases from building up and becoming a serious problem.

Earthing up Potatoes

An important aspect of potato growing, earthing (hilling) up protects potato tubers that are near the soil surface. If they are exposed to light, the tubers turn green and become inedible. When the green shoots are about 15cm (6in) tall, draw the soil up with a hoe on either side of the plants. Continue to do this as the potatoes grow, until the soil is mounded up to about 15cm (6in).

> **GARDENER'S TIP**
> Spray cuttings in a propagator with a fungicide to prevent mould.

> **THINGS TO DO**
> **IN THE KITCHEN GARDEN**
> Thin the fruit on gooseberry bushes
> Check gooseberry foliage for
> sawfly caterpillars
> Check strawberries for grey
> mould (botrytis)
> Feed asparagus plants after harvesting

Thinning Seedlings

Unless they are thinned now, vegetable seedlings will crowd each other out and crop poorly. The recommended distance for each crop will vary depending on the variety; check the seed packet for details. The uprooted seedlings of some crops can be used in salads.

Thin the emerging crops in stages. The first thinning should leave the plants twice as close as the final recommended spacing. Simply pull up the surplus plants with your finger and thumb and discard.

Above: Use a hoe to draw soil up around the developing potatoes without damaging the delicate root system.

Above: Thin seedlings to the distance recommended on the seed packet to give them space to develop properly.

24

THE GREENHOUSE

Summer is a time when you need to keep a watchful eye on your greenhouse and conservatory plants, which can easily overheat as the temperature rises outdoors.

If you have time and if there is space in the greenhouse, this is a good time to take softwood cuttings of shrubs from the open garden.

TAKING SOFTWOOD CUTTINGS

Softwood cuttings usually root readily, but need the warm, protected environment that glass provides. The method is suitable for many garden shrubs as well as conservatory plants.

1 Cut a sideshoot just above a bud. Trim just below a leaf joint and trim back the tip to leave a stem about 10cm (4in) long.

2 Using a dibber, insert up to two-thirds of the stem in a pot of cuttings potting mix.

3 Label the pot and tent with clear plastic supported on canes. Keep in shade, in the warmth of a heated propagator. Softwood cuttings should root in about 4–6 weeks.

THINGS TO DO
IN THE GREENHOUSE

Feed and water pot plants
Use biological controls to eliminate pests
Divide congested pot plants

SHRUBS TO INCREASE BY
SOFTWOOD CUTTINGS

Abutilon
Aloysia
Cotoneaster
Cytisus
Daphne
Fuchsia
Hydrangea
Philadelphus

25

Midsummer

FOR MOST GARDENERS THIS IS THE PEAK OF THE GARDENING YEAR, WHEN ALL YOUR EARLIER EFFORTS ARE REWARDED. THE FLOWER BORDERS ARE A RIOT OF COLOUR AND SCENT, AND THE VEGETABLE PLOT IS FILLED TO OVERFLOWING WITH FRESH YOUNG CROPS.

THE ORNAMENTAL GARDEN

On the hottest days of summer you will want to sit back and relax and enjoy your garden, but there are still plenty of jobs to be done if the garden is to continue looking good.

Above: Iris *'Blue Eyed Brunette' is one of the large number of rhizomatous irises that can be divided in midsummer.*

THINGS TO DO
IN THE ORNAMENTAL GARDEN
Divide flag irises
Take semi-ripe cuttings
Plant hardy cyclamen
Prune wisteria
Watch for and treat roses
for disease
Top up ponds in hot weather
Thin oxygenating plants in ponds

PLANTING AUTUMN CROCUSES

Corms of autumn crocus (*Colchicum autumnale*) can be planted in lawns, borders or even in the light shade of a deciduous tree. They will flower after two or three months, but the leaves will not appear until the following spring.

1 For an informal look, scatter the bulbs over grass and plant them where they land.

2 Use a bulb planter to take out a plug of soil. Place a corm in the base of each hole.

3 Remove a little soil from the bottom of the plug to allow for the depth of the corm. Replace the plug and firm in.

Above: Autumn crocuses, such as Colchicum *'The Giant', are not in fact crocuses, but resemble the spring flowers.*

DIVIDING IRISES

Rhizomatous irises can be divided immediately after they have flowered.

1 Lift the clump and cut away the old unproductive parts of the rhizome. Sections for replanting should have at least one growing point.

2 Replant the cut sections, ensuring the upper surface of the rhizome lies above the soil's surface. Trim back the topgrowth into a V-shape to minimize wind rock.

PLANTS TO INCREASE BY LAYERING

Aucuba
Campsis
Chaenomeles
Clematis
Erica
Humulus
Laurus
Lonicera
Magnolia
Rhododendron
Skimmia
Solanum
Wisteria

LAYERING

Woody shrubs and climbers with flexible stems can be increased by layering. This is a reliable method because the new plant remains attached to the parent while rooting takes place, but it is not usually practicable for producing more than a couple of plants. Layers can take up to a year to root, after which they can be severed from the parent plant.

1 Bring a flexible, low-growing branch (this is a rhododendron) down to ground level about 15–30cm (6–12in) from the tip.

2 Dig a shallow hole in the bed where the stem meets the ground and peg the stem in place. Cover with soil. Bend the tip of the stem as near to the vertical as possible and tie it loosely to a supporting cane, to encourage upright growth.

GARDENER'S TIP
Conserve water by installing water butts and mulch around plants to reduce evaporation from the soil surface.

Midsummer

The Kitchen Garden

This is a busy time in the kitchen garden. Plants must be watered regularly so that their growth is not checked, and weeds, which will compete for nutrients, must be removed as soon as they are noticed. If you are an organic gardener, this is a good time to apply a dilute seaweed foliar feed as a spray.

Controlling Weeds

Effective weed control is important throughout the growing season, but especially so now, when any weeds missed earlier on will be growing strongly, flowering and setting seed. Once you have got on top of the problem, use mulches to prevent weed seeds blown in from neighbouring gardens from germinating.

1 Chemical weedkillers can be useful for clearing a large area quickly. Choose a still day to apply them, to prevent them blowing on to neighbouring ornamental plants. Repeated applications may be necessary for tough weeds.

2 To remove taprooted weeds such as dandelions, loosen the soil around the weed with a fork before tugging it free. Sections of root left in the ground will regrow, so it is important to remove the whole plant.

3 Covering the soil around your vegetable crops with black plastic is unsightly, but it will prevent new weeds from appearing.

4 A layer of bark chippings or crushed cocoa shells is easier on the eye and can be spread around plants once all the weeds have been eliminated. Any weeds that germinate in the mulch itself should be removed promptly.

**THINGS TO DO
IN THE KITCHEN GARDEN**
Pinch out tips of runner beans when
they reach the required height
Cut back foliage on
fruited strawberries
Sow autumn and winter salads
Earth (hill) up celery
Harvest onions, garlic and shallots
Water vegetables during
dry weather

THE GREENHOUSE

As the temperature rises in the greenhouse, you may need to provide shade, either in the form of purpose-made blinds or by applying a special wash to the glass. On hot, sunny days, damping down by spraying the floor and staging first thing in the morning will improve the atmosphere.

CULTIVATING INDOOR TOMATOES

As they come into flower, the tomatoes growing in the greenhouse need regular attention if they are to produce the best crop. Look out, too, for early signs of pests and diseases and deal with these promptly.

1 If you are growing tall varieties, snap off any sideshoots as soon as they appear by pulling them sharply toward you. Do not remove sideshoots from bush varieties.

2 To ensure pollination in the greenhouse, shake the tomato plants each day or spray the flowers regularly with water to disperse the pollen.

3 Remove any yellowing leaves from the base of the plants.

4 After the plant has set between four and seven fruit trusses, stop the top of the plant by removing the growing tip. (The warmer the environment, the more trusses you can allow to ripen.)

Other Indoor Crops

Pinch out the growing tips on aubergine (eggplant) plants once they are about 30cm (12in) tall. Allow only one fruit to develop on each shoot. Count three leaves beyond the fruit then pinch out the tip of each shoot. Keep the atmosphere around the plants humid by regular misting.

Train the sideshoots of melon plants on to horizontal wires. To pollinate the flowers, transfer the pollen from the male to the female flowers using a small paintbrush. Pinch back the sideshoots to two leaves beyond each fruit that develops.

Pinch out male flowers on cucumbers to prevent pollination (which affects the flavour of the fruits). Many modern varieties have exclusively female flowers.

**THINGS TO DO
IN THE GREENHOUSE**

Care for tomato plants and other crops
under glass
Damp down the floor on hot days
Ventilate on hot days

Late Summer

SUMMER TRAVELS MAY MEAN THAT YOU HAVE TO BE AWAY FROM THE GARDEN WHEN IT NEEDS DAILY CARE. IT'S WORTH ASKING A NEIGHBOUR TO TAKE ON SOME OF THE LIGHTER TASKS, ESPECIALLY WATERING, AND OFFERING TO RETURN THE FAVOUR.

THE ORNAMENTAL GARDEN

This is often the hottest time of year, and you won't want to tackle a heavy workload. Above a certain temperature, plant growth stops anyway, and this year's growth on woody plants is now starting to firm up.

You need to keep a close eye on containers and hanging baskets, which can dry out all too quickly. Water

Above: Grouping containers together helps to shade the pots, keeping them cooler and conserving moisture.

them every day – twice a day if necessary – and remember that an evening watering is more economical, since the moisture will evaporate more slowly. You might also consider moving the containers to a position that is shaded at midday, to avoid leaf scorch.

Plants are rapidly forming seeds at this time, so remember to remove faded flowers promptly to keep up the flower power in containers and hanging baskets. In the open garden, however, this is a good time of year to harvest seed from any perennials and bulbs that you wish to increase. Cut off the flowerheads as soon as the seeds ripen but before they fall, and shake them into a paper bag for storage. Species are easily raised from seed (*Lilium regale* is especially rewarding), but hybrids will not come true.

THINGS TO DO
IN THE ORNAMENTAL GARDEN
Collect seed from annuals and perennials
Take cuttings of tender perennials
Dig up spent annuals
Layer carnations and pinks
Remove shed leaves from roses
Prune rambling roses
Trim hedges

Above: Collect seed by shaking it off the seedhead (here of an allium) into a paper bag. Store in a cool, dry place.

The garden can easily start to look tired after a prolonged hot spell. Cutting back flopping foliage on perennial plants such as artemisias and achilleas will usually promote a flush of new leaves, restoring freshness to your borders.

Rambling Roses

By now, rambling roses will have finished flowering and there should be plenty of vigorous shoots appearing near the base. Cut out the older stems and tie in the new ones while they are still flexible, training them horizontally to promote plenty of sideshoots.

This is a time of year when ramblers often fall victim to mildew and other fungal diseases, caused by poor air circulation through the plant and dryness at the roots. Keep plants well watered, especially if they are next to a wall where the soil may be dry.

PRUNING RAMBLERS

Opening up the topgrowth by pruning can help to revive congested ramblers and prevent disease.

1 Cut old flowered stems back to near ground level, reaching in to the base of the plant with loppers if necessary.

2 Tie in new shoots as close to the horizontal as possible, for flowering next year.

> **GARDENER'S TIP**
> Stop feeding roses and other shrubs, because a rush of new, lush growth will be susceptible to frost damage.

THE KITCHEN GARDEN

Regular watering and weeding in late summer will ensure that all your fruit and vegetables produce good crops.

Watering Systems

Although they can seem expensive luxuries, automatic watering systems that deliver water to the ground rather than spraying it around indiscriminately can save time, money and effort. They are especially useful if your vegetable plot is any distance from your outdoor tap and if your water is metered.

A simple seep or drip hose, which can be laid along a row of plants, will water the ground immediately under it and supply water to the roots of nearby plants. More sophisticated systems allow you to attach T-junctions so that several rows can be watered. Attaching a water timer or even a computer to the tap will give a completely automatic system.

**THINGS TO DO
IN THE KITCHEN GARDEN**

Summer-prune fruit trees
Support heavily laden fruit tree branches
Watch for viral diseases
Lift ripening marrows, pumpkins
and squashes on to straw
Pinch out tops of tomato plants

GARDENER'S TIP
If the weather turns damp, protect
drying onions with a cloche.

HARVESTING ONIONS

As the foliage on onion plants starts to wither, the bulbs can be lifted. Choose a warm spell of weather and allow the onions to ripen for a few days in the sun. They will harden and store better.

1 Bend over the topgrowth to expose as much of the bulb to the sun as possible.

2 When the foliage is straw-coloured, lift the onions and rest them on the surface for a few days. The roots should face the sun.

3 Finish off the hardening process by raising the onions on a mesh supported on bricks to allow good air circulation.

THE GREENHOUSE

As you empty plant pots and seed pans, make a point of washing them thoroughly before you store them. It is all too easy to put the used containers to one side and then to forget about them: they will be an ideal breeding ground for pests and diseases.

Bringing Cyclamen into Growth

Tender cyclamen (hybrids of *Cyclamen persicum*) that have been resting over summer can now be brought back into growth. Gently remove the tuber from its pot and rub off the old potting mix. Using fresh potting mix, pot the tuber on, so that the top is just above the potting mix surface. Put the pot in a well-lit position (but out of direct sunlight) no warmer than around 16°C (61°F). Water sparingly around the tuber, increasing the amounts as the plant comes into growth.

Above: The many unnamed hybrids of Cyclamen persicum *can be started into growth now to give a good winter display.*

PLANTING HYACINTHS FOR FORCING

Specially prepared hyacinth bulbs that will flower indoors in winter should now be appearing for sale. They will have been kept in controlled conditions that persuade the plants that winter is already well advanced. Plant them in specially formulated bulb fibre, which contains extra bark.

1 Plant the bulbs in a shallow container, close together but not touching.

2 Pack potting mix around the bulbs, leaving the noses (tops) exposed. Water gently. Keep the container in a cool, dark place and water just to keep the potting mix moist until the shoots are about 5cm (2in) high. Then bring them into a light position (but out of direct sunlight).

> ### THINGS TO DO
> ### IN THE GREENHOUSE
> Bring cyclamen into growth
> Sow seed for flowering pot
> plants, such as *Calceolaria*
> and *Schizanthus*

Early Autumn

AUTUMN IS THE SEASON FOR HARVESTING FRUITS FROM THE GARDEN. THE DAYS ARE GETTING COOLER AND SHORTER NOW, MAKING YOU MORE RELUCTANT TO LINGER IN THE GARDEN, BUT THIS IS A TIME TO PRESS ON WITH SEVERAL IMPORTANT TASKS.

THE ORNAMENTAL GARDEN

Traditionally, autumn is the time to plant hardy shrubs and trees, and conditions are usually ideal. The soil is still warm, but the days are shorter and cooler, making plants less likely to dry out. And the first frosts are still some weeks away.

**THINGS TO DO
IN THE ORNAMENTAL GARDEN**
Take cuttings of tender perennials
Sow hardy annuals for spring flowers
Clear summer bedding
Disbud dahlias and chrysanthemums
Lift gladioli and other tender bulbs

Above: The autumn display of Rosa *'Buff Beauty' is often even better than the summer one.*

Planning for Spring

Good gardeners are always looking ahead, and as soon as one group of plants starts to die back, they begin to think about what is going to replace them. Spent summer bedding plants can now make way for fresh plantings in preparation for the following spring. The soil is likely to be exhausted, so once the bed is cleared work in some general fertilizer and some organic matter to improve structure.

PLANTING SPRING BEDDING

Early-flowering bedding plants such as wallflowers (*Erysimum*) and forget-me-nots (*Myosotis*) can be interplanted with bulbs such as tulips for a colourful spring display.

1 Spring bedding plants are often sold at this time of year in modules, unless you have managed to grow your own. Space them evenly across the bed.

2 Once all the bedding plants are in, drop the bulbs among them and plant them using a slim trowel. Most bulbs should be planted so that they are covered with twice their own depth of soil.

Lifting Gladioli

In mild areas gladioli may still be flowering in early autumn, but in colder districts you will need to lift the corms for storage over the winter before they can be nipped by the first hard frosts.

As the topgrowth starts to die back, lift the corms with a fork. Trim off most of the foliage to leave just a stub. Dry the corms off for a few days in a well-ventilated place.

Snap off the tiny new corms that you will find around the base of the main corm. You can either discard these or keep them for growing on (they will take several years to reach flowering size). Dust the large corms with fungicide and store them in paper bags in a dry, frost-free environment for re-planting next spring.

Above: After flowering, lift gladioli corms and store them in a dry, frost-free place. This is Gladiolus *'Charming Beauty'.*

THE KITCHEN GARDEN

There are a number of leafy vegetables that can be sown now for winter crops. Look for lettuce varieties that have been bred for autumn sowing, and try sowing lamb's lettuce (mâche), rocket (arugula) and winter purslane as cold month crops. Spring cabbages sown now will provide spring greens early next year. Cover seedlings with a cloche if the weather turns cold.

Lifting Root Vegetables

Beetroot (beets), carrots and turnips can be lifted now for storing over winter. Only undamaged roots are suitable for storing. Twist off the leaves and pack the roots in wooden boxes filled with sand. Keep the root vegetables in

Above: Beetroot (beets), here grown in a raised bed, is best harvested while quite small, about seven weeks after sowing.

a cool but frost-free place. Parsnips and swedes should be left in the ground until after the first frosts, as this improves their flavour.

Above: Globe artichokes will be ready for harvesting in early autumn of the second year after planting. They should be eaten as soon as possible after cutting.

PROTECTING OUTDOOR TOMATOES

It is likely that outdoor tomatoes will still be ripening. Green fruits can be picked and ripened indoors provided they are reasonably mature, but for the best flavour it makes sense to ripen as many as possible on the plant. They will benefit from some protection, particularly if frosts are forecast. Plants trained to vertical stakes can be tented with horticultural fleece. Alternatively, the plants can be untied and rested on the ground.

2 Cover the tomatoes with a rigid plastic cloche, which will warm the air around them – thus speeding up ripening – as well as keeping off frost.

1 Untie the plants from their stakes. To avoid any damage to the fruit and provide a little extra insulation, spread a layer of dry straw on the ground and gently lower the plants on to this.

3 Alternatively, cover the plants loosely with horticultural fleece. This protects against frost but will not warm up the air to the same extent as a rigid cloche.

THINGS TO DO
IN THE KITCHEN GARDEN
Protect outdoor tomatoes
against frost
Plant strawberries
Stake Brussels sprouts
Divide herbaceous herbs

GARDENER'S TIP
Sow a crop of green manure (such as mustard) to use up nutrients left in vacant ground after harvesting. It will be recycled when the crop is dug in.

THE GREENHOUSE

Before the first autumn frosts, take time to make sure that any heating system in your greenhouse is in good working order. Check that all extension leads are in good condition and take any heaters to be serviced if you are not confident of your own abilities to look after them.

Plants now need all the light they can get, so remove any greenhouse blinds or shading. If you applied a shading wash earlier in the year, it can usually be rubbed off with a cloth when the glass is dry.

Sowing Hardy Annuals

If you want an early display of flowers next season, hardy annuals can be sown now for planting out next

Above: Continue to keep the greenhouse well ventilated. Even in autumn you will find that the temperature under the glass will rise sharply on a sunny day.

spring. They can also be grown on in pots to provide flowering pot plants for the conservatory. Compact forms of pot marigolds (*Calendula*) are easy and rewarding, or try cornflowers, godetias or stocks (*Matthiola*).

Protecting Early-flowering Shrubs

If you grow early-flowering shrubs, such as daphnes, skimmias or camellias, in pots, move them under cover for earlier, perfectly formed flowers. Keep them well-watered and in good light, but check that they do not scorch on the odd sunny day when the temperature can rise dramatically.

Bringing in Houseplants

Many winter- and spring-flowering houseplants, such as zygocactus, solanums grown for their winter berries and even orchids, benefit from spending the summer outdoors, but they must be brought inside before the first frost threatens. Remove any fallen leaves and debris from the soil surface and clean the pots carefully to avoid contaminating the greenhouse. Check for any signs of disease and look under the leaves for snails and other pests before bringing them in.

REPOTTING CACTI

Cacti and succulents can be repotted at any time of year, but it is often convenient to do so either in spring or autumn. Cacti benefit from a specially formulated potting mix that allows very free drainage while supplying the correct nutrients. They also demand special handling.

1 Wrap the cactus in a length of cloth or thick paper to protect your hands from the spines. Ease it from the container.

2 Centre the plant in the new container and fill the sides with cactus potting mix.

3 Top-dress with a handful of grit to improve drainage and to protect the collar of the plant from excess moisture. Withhold water for several days to allow any damaged roots to form calluses.

THINGS TO DO
IN THE GREENHOUSE

Bring in houseplants that have spent
the summer outdoors
Sow seed of spring-flowering
tender perennials
Clean off summer shading washes
Pot up and pot on seedlings of
pot plants as necessary
Check greenhouse heating system

Mid-autumn

AT THIS TIME OF YEAR YOU NEED TO BE ALERT TO SUDDEN CHANGES IN THE WEATHER. IN A BALMY SPELL, PLANTS WILL CONTINUE TO GROW AND SOME MAY EVEN FLOWER, BUT A COLD NIGHT OR TWO WILL SOON REMIND YOU THAT WINTER IS JUST AROUND THE CORNER.

THE ORNAMENTAL GARDEN

If you need to lay a new lawn and did not do so in spring, consider ordering turfs or sowing seed now. The soil will still be warm enough to encourage the roots to grow strongly and there will be plenty of autumn rain.

If your established lawn is looking rather tired and bedraggled, autumn is the time for tasks such as scarifying, to remove an accumulation of clippings, and spiking, to aerate the soil. Sweep up all fallen leaves, which can damage the lawn. They should be collected to make leaf mould, a precious organic substance that can be used either as a mulch or as a general soil improver.

Pond Care

Garden ponds – especially informal and wildlife ones – generally look after themselves, but most repay a little extra attention at this time of year. There is always the danger that leaves shed by deciduous shrubs and trees, as well as other plant debris, will find their way into the water. If left there, they will rot and create poisonous gases. Either net the pond to catch any debris, or rake the surface to collect any fallen leaves.

Above: Osteospermums are not reliably hardy, but they have a long flowering season and will bloom until the first frosts. This is Osteospermum 'Lady Leitrim'.

Pruning Deciduous Shrubs

Although hard pruning should be left until spring, you can cut back whippy growth on tall deciduous shrubs, such as buddlejas and some roses, to prevent wind rock. Reduce the topgrowth by up to one third.

Beds and Borders

Plants of doubtful hardiness, such as fuchsias, osteospermums, busy Lizzies and *Begonia semperflorens*, can be dug up now for storage over winter. Fuchsias should be kept dry, but the others can be kept growing in a warm, light place, where they will continue to flower for a few more weeks.

Lifting and Storing Dahlias

Dahlias are not hardy, but they should be left in the ground until a hard frost has blackened the topgrowth. The tubers can then be lifted for storage over winter.

1 When the foliage turns black, cut back the topgrowth to about 15cm (6in) above the ground and remove any stakes. Lift the tubers with a fork.

2 Carefully rub off as much soil as possible. Leave the tubers to dry off in an airy place such as a shed or unheated greenhouse. Store in paper bags in a cool but frost-free place over winter.

Planting a Root-balled Conifer

Root-balled conifers are lifted from the nursery field in autumn, and should be planted as soon as possible. Prepare a planting hole of the correct depth and width to accommodate the roots (check the depth with a cane) and remove the covering from the roots. Backfill with the excavated soil and firm in well. Keep the conifer well watered during dry spells and shelter it from winter gales, which could dry out the foliage.

Above: Place a cane across the hole to make sure that trees and shrubs are planted to their original depth.

**THINGS TO DO
IN THE ORNAMENTAL GARDEN**
Plant spring bulbs (except tulips)
Plant bare-root roses and other shrubs
Lift and store dahlias
Plant spring bedding
Divide herbaceous plants
Bring tender perennials under cover
Plant new hedging
Scarify and spike established lawns

THE KITCHEN GARDEN

Taking steps to protect your plants from frost will keep them in good condition in case it turns cold before you are ready to harvest them. The stems of vegetables such as celery and beetroot (beets) can be protected with straw. Bend the surrounding leaves over the heads of late cauliflowers. Other vulnerable vegetables can be sheltered under cloches.

LIFTING AND STORING POTATOES

Late potatoes are mainly grown for use during the winter, and should now be ready for harvesting and storing. Small crops can be kept indoors, but if space is at a premium, consider making a potato clamp in a sheltered spot in the garden.

2 Sort the potatoes by size, as the largest tubers are the most suitable for winter storage. The tiniest potatoes should be used immediately if you wish, otherwise they can be discarded. You should be able to sort the remainder into three groups: small, for early consumption, medium and large, for storing indoors or in a potato clamp in the garden.

1 Once the foliage has died down, lift the potatoes with a fork, though they can be left longer as long as frost does not threaten. Leave them on the soil surface for a few hours to harden off the outer skins.

3 Place the larger potatoes in sacks and store them in a dark, cool, but frost-free place. Paper sacks are best, but if you cannot obtain these, use plastic sacks, making slits to provide some ventilation.

4 To make a potato clamp, excavate a shallow depression in bare soil and line it with a thick layer of dry straw. Pile the potatoes on top. Heap another layer of straw over the top of the potatoes, thick enough to provide good insulation. Mound the excavated earth over the straw, but leave a few tufts protruding to ensure adequate ventilation in the clamp. The tubers will be protected from all but the most severe weather.

Caring for Fruit Trees

Pick apples when they are ripe, which is usually when the fruit comes away easily with a quick twist of the wrist. Store sound fruit in a cool, dark place, ensuring the fruits do not touch.

Clear away fallen fruit and leaves from around fruit trees. If this debris is left on the ground it tends to harbour pests and diseases ready to attack the trees next spring. Fasten grease bands around the trunks of fruit trees so that wingless female codling moths cannot climb up the trunks to lay eggs.

> **THINGS TO DO**
> **IN THE KITCHEN GARDEN**
> Plant spring cabbages
> Earth (hill) up celery and leek plants
> Lift and store potatoes
> Protect vulnerable vegetables
> with cloches
> Pot up herbs for winter use
> Harvest and store apples
> Cut spent canes of summer-fruiting
> raspberries to the ground
> Protect late-fruiting strawberries
> from frost
> Apply grease bands to apple trees

Protecting Herbs

You can keep some of your herbs, including parsley, cropping throughout the winter if you protect them from frosts with a rigid plastic cloche. Make sure the end pieces are tightly secured to keep out the cold, but remove the cloche on warm, dry days.

Above: Rigid plastic cloches are ideal for protecting herbs such as parsley throughout the winter months.

THE GREENHOUSE

As the weather turns damper, you need to keep a look out for fungal problems, such as grey mould (botrytis). Good ventilation should minimize the risk, but this becomes less easy as the outdoor temperature drops. Remove dead, faded or diseased-looking leaves from plants and burn them. Spray the plants with copper fungicide solution. If you decide to use fumigation to control any pests and diseases that are lingering, read the manufacturer's instructions before use because some types can be used only in completely empty greenhouses.

Above: *If you can manage to empty your greenhouse completely, you can make sure that you rid it of all lurking pests and diseases by fumigating it.*

Above: *Lily-of-the-valley (*Convallaria majalis*) can be potted up in mid-autumn for growing on under glass to provide winter flowers.*

Forcing Lily-of-the-valley

For fragrant early flowers, force some lily-of-the-valley (*Convallaria majalis*) under glass. Dig up or buy a few rhizomes (sometimes known as pips) and pot them up. The more heat you can provide, the earlier they will flower. Although they can be planted out after flowering, they may take a season or two to regain their vigour and to flower as usual. Do not try to force the same rhizomes again.

STORING PELARGONIUMS

Pelargoniums that have flowered their hearts out in summer borders will now be performing less well. They can be lifted from the ground this month and stored over winter, either for replanting next year or to provide material for early cuttings.

1 Lift the pelargoniums from the ground before the first frost if possible, though they will often survive a light frost if you take them in promptly afterwards. Shake off as much soil from the roots as possible.

2 Trim back the longest roots and shorten the shoots to about 10cm (4in).

3 Pot up the plants in 15cm (6in) deep trays or pots of soil or sowing compost. Water them well initially, but sparingly over winter, just to prevent the soil from drying out. New shoots will emerge in spring, from which you can take cuttings.

> **THINGS TO DO IN THE GREENHOUSE**
> Continue to ventilate in mild weather
> Install a thermometer to check minimum temperatures at night
> Remove and burn any dead or diseased leaves from plants
> Clean and disinfect work areas

Late Autumn

THIS TIME OF YEAR OFTEN SPRINGS A SURPRISE: ALTHOUGH COLD, THE DAYS CAN BE CLEAR AND SUNNY. TAKE A STROLL ROUND THE GARDEN AND NOTE ANY DESIGN FEATURES THAT NEED IMPROVEMENT. NOW IS THE TIME TO GET THE GARDEN READY FOR WINTER.

THE ORNAMENTAL GARDEN

If you like a tidy garden, begin to cut back herbaceous perennials to about 15cm (6in) above the ground as the foliage and flowers die back.

Some gardeners prefer to leave the dead topgrowth in place until spring because it protects the crowns from winter cold. In addition, many plants, especially grasses, look attractive when their dry leaves and flowerheads are touched with frost. Seedheads left on plants such as teasels (*Dipsacus fullonum*) provide valuable winter food for birds, as do the insects that overwinter inside dead stems. However, garden pests, including slugs and snails, will also overwinter among the dead plant material, and it can be difficult to avoid damaging the tender new growth when you are cutting back the old topgrowth in spring.

Bulbs in Beds and Borders

As nerines start to die back after flowering, mulch them with straw or some other dry material if you live in a cold area. This is a good time to divide congested clumps, but do this only if the plants have ceased to flower well.

Above: Spiraea japonica 'Goldflame' is one of the shrubs that can be propagated from hardwood cuttings taken about now.

Nerines are best left well alone as far as possible, but some other tender bulbs, such as gladioli, should be lifted so that they can be stored in a dry, frost-free place until next spring. There is still time to plant spring-flowering bulbs, including tulips.

> GARDENER'S TIP
> If you plan a bonfire, either warn your neighbours or light it in the evening when you are least likely to cause inconvenience.

46

TAKING HARDWOOD CUTTINGS

You can increase your stock of a wide range of trees and shrubs by taking hardwood cuttings. They occupy little space, and aftercare is minimal, though they take up to a year to root.

1 Dig a narrow trench about 20cm (8in) deep. If the soil is heavy, line the base with a 2.5cm (1in) layer of grit or sharp sand. Take cuttings from the plant, each of which should have four or more buds. Trim the base of each cutting just below a bud and the top just above a bud.

> **SHRUBS TO INCREASE BY HARDWOOD CUTTINGS**
> *Aucuba*
> *Berberis*
> *Buddleja*
> *Buxus*
> *Cornus*
> *Cotoneaster*
> *Escallonia*
> *Forsythia*
> *Kerria*
> *Philadelphus*
> *Rosa*
> *Salix*
> *Spiraea*
> *Weigela*

2 Insert the cuttings in the trench, making sure they are the right way up. Two or three buds should protrude above the ground, although if you are taking cuttings from a single-stemmed tree, you should insert them to their full length so that the topmost bud is just below the soil surface.

3 Firm in the cuttings, label them and water them in well. Leave them undisturbed until the following autumn, by which time they should have rooted.

Above: Plant tulip bulbs to a depth of 8–15cm (3–6in). Tulipa praestans 'Fusilier' has up to six flowers on each stem.

> **THINGS TO DO IN THE ORNAMENTAL GARDEN**
> Cut back perennials
> Burn woody garden debris
> Plant bare-root roses and other shrubs
> Plant tulip bulbs
> Take hardwood cuttings
> Plant hedges
> Collect and compost fallen leaves
> Protect vulnerable plants by packing around them with straw

The Kitchen Garden

As you clear the vegetable plot of the last of the summer crops, dig over the soil and leave it so that winter frosts can break down large clods. This is especially important if your soil is heavy. Continue to protect vulnerable plants with cloches or straw.

Planting Soft Fruit

Traditionally, soft fruit bushes are sold at this time of year as bare-root plants, and they should be planted as soon after purchase as possible, while they are dormant. Container-grown plants can be planted at any time of year when the weather is suitable and the ground is not waterlogged or frozen, although these, too, are best planted at this time of year.

1 Dig a large hole for each plant and work organic matter into the base. Soak the plant roots in a bucket of water for at least an hour and then place them in the centre of the hole. Use a cane to make sure you are planting at the original depth.

2 Backfill with the excavated soil and firm in well with your foot to eliminate pockets of air. Hoe around the plant to remove your footprints, then water the plant well.

3 Soft fruits that grow on stems that sprout from the base should be pruned hard. Cut back the topgrowth to about 23–30cm (9–12in) from ground level to stimulate new shoots from the base.

> ### THINGS TO DO
> ### IN THE KITCHEN GARDEN
> Protect vulnerable vegetables
> with cloches
> Plant bare-root fruit bushes and trees
> Prune soft fruit bushes
> Pot up herbs for winter use

Pruning Soft Fruit

Once established, soft fruit bushes need pruning while dormant to maintain their vigour. Blackcurrants should be pruned only once they are fruiting reliably. Cut back one third of the shoots to the base, choosing the oldest. Red and white currants fruit on wood that is two or more years old, so pruning should concentrate on removing overcrowded shoots. Shorten sideshoots to one or two buds, and on main shoots cut back last summer's growth by half. Gooseberries also benefit from annual pruning to keep an open shape.

Autumn-fruiting raspberries bear fruit on the new season's canes, so all canes can be cut to ground level during the dormant season. On summer-fruiting varieties, the old canes that have fruited should be removed and the new shoots tied in to replace them.

Planting Garlic

To grow successfully, garlic needs a period of cold and can be planted throughout the autumn until early winter. Although it is possible to grow garlic from cloves bought for cooking, you will get better results from specially produced bulbs.

Snap each bulb into its component cloves and plant them in a row in a sunny spot, up to 10cm (4in) apart and with the tips of the cloves just below the soil surface.

Above: *When frost is forecast, protect crops such as strawberries with a portable plastic cloche.*

> GARDENER'S TIP
> Pot up herbs such as mint, chives and marjoram, and keep them in the greenhouse or kitchen to ensure a supply of fresh leaves throughout the winter.

Above: *Use a dibber to make holes for garlic cloves, spacing them about 10cm (4in) apart along the row.*

THE GREENHOUSE

As the temperature drops, you need to start thinking about heating and insulation. Most conservatories are heated by means of the domestic system, but if your greenhouse is free-standing and has no power supply, you may consider installing a small gas or paraffin heater. These can be used only in a properly ventilated environment, however, because of the risk of fire or a build-up of noxious fumes.

Good insulation will help save on fuel bills. Bubble plastic is cheap and can be fixed to the greenhouse roof with clips. If you installed blinds or netting for shade in summer, you may be able to use the same fixings to hold the insulation in place.

If you have a large greenhouse that would be costly to heat, you may be

Above: An electric fan heater, especially if it is fitted with a thermostat, is an efficient way of heating a greenhouse.

able to group all the most tender plants together at one end and close this section off with a curtain of bubble plastic. Heat this area only.

Hygiene

If you have not already done so, take the opportunity to give the greenhouse a thorough clean before putting the insulation in place. If you used blinds or netting to shade the greenhouse during the summer, wash them before storing them away.

Clear away all dead and dying foliage and flowers so that grey mould (botrytis) cannot overwinter on the debris. Use hot water and a garden disinfectant or non-toxic detergent to clean the glass inside and out, taking particular care to clean between overlapping panes of glass, where algal growths tend to form. Also scrub down all wooden or metal frames and clean the staging.

Above: Insulate the greenhouse with sheets of bubble plastic fixed against the glass on the inside.

Before storing all your containers, plant pots and drip saucers over the winter, make sure they are clean, and wipe the outside of all containers used for long-term plants with a dilute solution of garden disinfectant.

Cold Frames

Although a cold frame is usually designed to store hardy plants, bear in mind that the plants will be young – and therefore more vulnerable than mature ones – and that their roots are above ground level: potting mix in pots can easily freeze in severe weather.

Above: Clean the greenhouse glass both inside and out to maximize light levels and to prevent the build-up of algae.

On the coldest nights, cover the frame with old carpet to protect from frost. Keep the carpet on in the daytime if the temperature stays below freezing. Excluding the light in very cold weather will do the plants no harm.

Above: Scrub all your plant pots and containers when not in use, so that they do not harbour disease.

> **THINGS TO DO
> IN THE GREENHOUSE**
> Clean all surfaces
> Clean greenhouse glass
> Insulate, if necessary
> Ventilate on mild days
> Check on indoor cyclamen and
> remove any dead leaves

Early Winter

THERE ARE STILL SOME ESSENTIAL GARDEN TASKS TO BE DONE IN WINTER, BUT THERE IS MUCH TO ENJOY AS WELL. AT THIS TIME OF YEAR THE VALUE OF EVERGREENS AND CONIFERS AS THE BACKBONE OF THE GARDEN CAN BE FULLY APPRECIATED.

THE ORNAMENTAL GARDEN

Continue to sweep up fallen leaves, especially from the lawn, and use them to make leaf mould.

One of the few perennials to be in flower at this time of year, the Christmas rose (*Helleborus niger*) can be difficult to keep looking its best. It often flowers during the worst of the winter weather, and it is worth protecting the emerging flower buds from rain and mud splashes. Alpines will also appreciate protection from winter wet, which is more likely to kill them than cold weather.

THE KITCHEN GARDEN

There will still be plenty of tidying up to do, as you clear away the last of this year's crops and dig over vacant beds to prepare for next season.

Pruning Apple and Pear Trees

Give some attention to apple and pear trees now that they are dormant. Pruning is largely a matter of tidying them up. Thin older branches to open up the crown and cut back any damaged branches entirely. If any growth shows signs of fungal disease such as mildew, cut back to firm, healthy

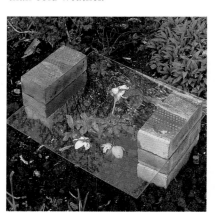

Above: A sheet of glass placed over Helleborus niger *will keep mud splashes off the pure white flowers.*

Above: Established apple cordons should be pruned in both winter and summer, but standards can be pruned in winter only.

wood and burn the prunings. Use a pruning saw with a serrated edge to deal with thicker branches. Take care that you do not prune too many branches too hard, as this will result in an excess of thin, sappy growth the following spring.

THE GREENHOUSE

On mild days make a point of opening the door or the roof lights to ventilate the greenhouse, and remove any fallen leaves or flowers. Reduce the water you give to plants that are being over-wintered in the greenhouse.

CHECKING STORED BULBS

If you are storing the dried bulbs, corms, tubers and rhizomes of such plants as freesias, gladioli, dahlias and begonias, it is worth checking up on them from time to time to make sure they are not showing any signs of rot.

1 About once a month, gently squeeze the bulbs (these are begonia tubers) to make sure they are still firm. Any that feel soft, or are showing signs of mould, should be discarded at once.

2 For extra protection, dust the healthy bulbs or tubers with a fungicidal powder, following the safety measures stipulated on the product label.

THINGS TO DO

Ornamental Garden
Sow seed of alpines
Put cloches over *Helleborus niger*
Protect alpines from winter wet
Install a pond heater

Kitchen Garden
Prune apple and pear trees
Force witloof chicory

Greenhouse
Inspect bulbs in storage
Prune grape vines
Sow seed of pelargoniums

GARDENER'S TIP
Clean and oil your lawn mower now, as you are unlikely to have time when it is in regular use in summer, or take it to be professionally serviced before the busy spring season.

Midwinter

AT THIS TIME OF YEAR YOU NEED TO START LOOKING FORWARD. NO MATTER HOW COLD THE WEATHER, SPRING IS ONLY JUST AROUND THE CORNER. NOW IS THE TIME TO PLAN YOUR PLANTING SCHEMES, ORDER SEEDS AND CHECK THAT YOUR TOOLS ARE IN GOOD REPAIR.

THE ORNAMENTAL GARDEN

A job that is easily overlooked at this time of year is to knock off snow from the tops of hedges and specimen conifers. Evergreen hedges are usually trimmed so that the top slopes slightly, encouraging snow to slide off. Sometimes, however, heavy snowfall can lie on branches, causing permanent damage.

TAKING ROOT CUTTINGS

Root cuttings are an excellent way of increasing stocks of a number of perennials, but the plant must be fully dormant for the technique to be successful. Keep the cuttings in a cold frame or unheated greenhouse. New growth should appear in spring, when the young plants can be potted up individually and grown on for a season.

PLANTS TO INCREASE BY
ROOT CUTTINGS
Acanthus
Echinops
Gaillardia
Phlox maculata
Phlox paniculata
Pulsatilla vulgaris
Romneya coulteri

---

1 Dig up the plant when it is dormant and remove some of the thicker roots, cutting close to the crown. Replant the crown.

2 Cut the roots into 5cm (2in) sections. Angle the cut at the base of each one to show the correct way up. Insert vertically in pots of cuttings potting mix.

3 For plants with thin roots, such as border phlox, lay 5cm (2in) lengths of root in pots of potting mix. Cover with a fairly thin layer of potting mix.

THINGS TO DO
IN THE ORNAMENTAL GARDEN
Firm in new plantings lifted by frost
Check the stakes on trees
Prune wisteria
Aerate lawns
Melt ice on ponds

The Kitchen Garden

While most of the vegetable plot is bare, take the opportunity to test the soil. Most vegetables do best in slightly alkaline soil, so if necessary apply lime, in the form of calcium carbonate or calcium hydroxide (slaked lime), following the supplier's directions precisely.

Forcing Rhubarb

If you grow rhubarb, cover some of the crowns with a large bucket or a special rhubarb forcer that excludes light. This will encourage early growth that is pale, thin and tender – excellent for pies and fools in spring.

For a really early crop of rhubarb, lift the crown to expose the roots and leave it on the soil surface for a few weeks. This will persuade the plant that winter is more advanced than it really is and bring it into growth earlier. Replant the crown and cover the emerging shoots.

Above: Check stored apples regularly and promptly remove any fruits that show signs of rot.

Forcing Chicory

Chicory roots are sometimes sold at this time of year for forcing to produce chicons. Leave the roots on the soil surface for a few days to retard growth. Trim back the tops to leave stumps 2.5–5cm (1–2in) long and pot them up in threes, leaving the crowns exposed (trim the roots if necessary to fit in the pot). Cover with a second pot with the holes blocked to exclude light and keep at a temperature of 10–18°C (50–65°F). The chicons will be ready to cut in about three weeks.

> **THINGS TO DO**
> **IN THE KITCHEN GARDEN**
> Net fruit bushes to protect emerging
> buds from birds
> Force rhubarb and chicory
> Sow broad (fava) beans and peas
> (mild areas only)

THE GREENHOUSE

If you have a heated greenhouse or a heated propagator, it is not too soon to sow some summer bedding plants that need a long growing period, such as fibrous-rooted begonias *(Begonia semperflorens)*. Check seed packets to see if early sowings are needed.

It can be tempting to make early sowings of all half-hardy annuals and summer vegetables. However, remember that you will need plenty of space to keep the pricked-out and potted-on seedlings warm and well lit before they can be planted out. Seedlings that are kept in overcrowded, poorly ventilated conditions are susceptible to damping off, so in a small greenhouse it is more sensible to put off most early sowings for a few weeks.

Above: Now is the time to plan for next summer's chrysanthemum display. This is the early-flowering 'Primrose Allouise'.

PROPAGATING CHRYSANTHEMUMS

Chrysanthemums that are overwintered in a greenhouse or cold frame are generally used to produce new plants once they start into growth. In order to ensure large, robust plants for summer flowering, take cuttings from your stock plants now, once the new shoots reach about 5cm (2in).

1 Cut off shoots coming directly from the base of the plant. Pull off the lowest leaves and trim the base of each cutting.

2 Insert the stems around the edge of a pot containing a mixture suitable for cuttings.

3 Either tent the cuttings to raise the humidity or place them in a propagator. If you use a plastic bag, make sure that the plastic does not touch the leaves.

Bringing Hippeastrums into Growth

Bulbs of hippeastrums, which are often, misleadingly, sold as amaryllis, can be obtained at this time of year for indoor display. Plant the bulbs in pots of bulb fibre or potting mix with the top half of the bulb above the surface. If the bulb is slow to start into growth, place the pot in a propagator for a week or so until the first green shoots appear.

GARDENER'S TIP
To make tiny seed like begonia easier to handle and see, mix it with a small quantity of silver sand and sprinkle the sand and seed mix over the surface of the tray.

THINGS TO DO IN THE GREENHOUSE
Pick off and burn dead leaves from pot plants
Check stored corms and tubers for signs of rot
Continue to ventilate on mild days
Sow seed of annuals for early flowers

Above: Exotic-looking hippeastrums, such as this variety called 'Christmas Star', grow with phenomenal speed indoors, and bloom in the depths of winter.

Late Winter

THIS IS OFTEN WHEN THE WORST OF THE WINTER WEATHER STRIKES, BUT THE DAYS ARE BECOMING PERCEPTIBLY LONGER AND MANY OF THE SPRING BULBS ARE BEGINNING TO SHOOT FROM BELOW GROUND. THE AIR OF ANTICIPATION IS ALMOST PALPABLE.

THE ORNAMENTAL GARDEN

There is plenty to do in the garden at this time of year – and plenty to enjoy. Magnolia buds are fattening up, and many winter-flowering shrubs are at their best. Several have bewitching fragrances, and a few cut stems will scent the whole house.

Prune late-flowering clematis hard back to a pair of strong, healthy buds. Thinner stems that show no signs of shooting can be cut down completely.

Above: When you prune a clematis, cut each stem back to a pair of strong buds near ground level.

Summer bulbs will be appearing for sale. If you are buying lilies, look for firm, plump bulbs that show no sign of disease and plant them as soon as possible, adding grit or sharp sand to the soil to ensure good drainage. Dahlia tubers should be stored until the weather warms up in late spring.

Above: One of the first bulbs to appear, Crocus tommasinianus *is ideal for naturalizing in grass.*

THINGS TO DO
IN THE ORNAMENTAL GARDEN
Sow sweet peas
Plant snowdrops and winter aconites
immediately after flowering
Prune clematis
Divide overcrowded snowdrops
Take root cuttings of perennials
with thick, fleshy roots
Prepare ground for new lawns

THE KITCHEN GARDEN

Unless the soil is waterlogged or frozen, continue to dig over the vegetable plot, but take care that you do not compact wet soil by standing on it. Apply a mulch of well-rotted compost or manure to prevent weeds from germinating in the bare soil.

SOWING EARLY CROPS

If you have a cold frame erected directly over garden soil, take advantage of the few extra degrees of warmth it provides to sow some early crops. In the open garden, you can warm up patches of soil for early sowings with cloches of various kinds.

2 Rigid cloches made of polycarbon are useful for warming up small areas of the kitchen garden. Butt the sections close together and make sure they are firmly fixed in the ground. Close the ends with further sections of polycarbon to prevent the cloche becoming a wind tunnel.

3 You can warm up a larger area of soil with plastic sheeting stretched over metal or plastic hoops – an ambitious tunnel will have enough headroom to allow you to walk in and out of it. Pull the sheeting taut and secure it firmly at each end. Anchor the edges of the plastic to the ground by heaping soil over them.

1 If your cold frame is standing on bare soil, prepare the ground for sowing by forking it over and adding as much organic matter matter as possible. Well-rotted farmyard manure is useful for enriching the soil for early crops. More powerful artificial fertilizers are not recommended at this time. Rake the soil level and sow the seed thinly in shallow drills.

> ### THINGS TO DO
> ### IN THE KITCHEN GARDEN
> Continue winter digging
> Force young strawberry plants
> for an early crop
> Sprout early potatoes
> Feed asparagus beds
> Plant out Jerusalem artichokes
> Sow vegetables under cloches
> for early crops

THE GREENHOUSE

Make the most of your greenhouse, conservatory or kitchen windowsill to begin sowing seed of early vegetables and half-hardy annuals. To maximize the light that gets to your seedlings, make sure that the glass is clean. Don't forget to ventilate the greenhouse on warm days.

If you have stored dahlia tubers over winter, they can now be coaxed out of their dormancy. A good way of increasing your stock is to take cuttings from the emerging shoots. Provided you give them the appropriate care and attention, they should flower the same year.

For flowers in early summer, press on and sow seeds of annuals. A propagator can speed up germination, which is especially useful for half-hardy plants. To produce sturdy, healthy plants, prick them out as they grow. Early sowings can also be used to provide flowering pot plants for indoor displays.

Have a look at tender perennials you have overwintered, which will be mostly woody plants, such as fuchsias, pelargoniums, argyranthemums and felicias. Spraying them with water can help encourage them to push out fresh shoots. If the plants are old and straggly, any such shoots can be used as cuttings, if you didn't take cuttings the previous autumn.

Young plants need tender loving care. Keep them warm, in good light and out of draughts, and make sure they never dry out. If you need to keep

Above: Dahlia tubers that have been stored over the winter should be showing signs of growth now, and you can take cuttings to increase your stocks.

them in a closed environment such as a propagator, check regularly for signs of fungal disease, usually the result of excessive moisture.

Check that you have good supplies of clean pots and seed trays, potting mix for both seed and cuttings, and plant labels. You can save time later by stocking up now. Days that are too cold or wet for you to venture outside will be well spent washing old pots and sorting out seed packets.

GROWING CACTI FROM SEED

As a change, try growing cacti from seed, which is a gratifyingly easy way of producing large numbers of these fascinating plants. Use a heated propagator to start them off, then grow them on under normal greenhouse conditions but maintaining a minimum temperature of 10°C (50°F).

1 Fill small pots or a seed tray with seed potting mix or a potting mix specially formulated for cacti. Scatter the seed evenly and thinly over the surface.

2 Top-dress with a thin layer of fine gravel, water the pots or trays and stand them in a place that is warm and bright, but out of direct sunlight.

3 Prick the seedlings out when they are large enough to handle and pot them up. Most cacti do best in pots that are quite small in proportion to their topgrowth.

> **THINGS TO DO**
> **IN THE GREENHOUSE**
> Take cuttings of dahlias
> Bring overwintered tender perennials
> back into growth
> Sow tomatoes
> Ventilate on mild days
> Sow cacti

Glossary

aerate To improve the drainage of a lawn by spiking the surface, using either a garden fork or a special implement, to make a series of small holes.

annual A plant that completes its life cycle (from seed, to flowering, to setting seed and dying) within a single growing season. *See also* BIENNIAL.

biennial A plant, such as a foxglove (*Digitalis*), that completes its life cycle over two growing seasons. *See also* ANNUAL.

biological control A method of controlling pests involving the introduction of a natural predator into a greenhouse or the garden.

botrytis *See* GREY MOULD.

bud (1) An unopened flower. (2) The point (also called a node) on the woody stem of a plant from which new growth arises.

bulb An underground storage organ that allows a plant to return to a state of dormancy in order to survive extremes of temperature.

cloche Any movable, transparent or semi-transparent structure that provides temporary shelter to plants in the garden.

cold frame A small, enclosed outdoor structure used to protect young plants or to acclimatize plants to outdoor growing conditions.

corm A modified underground stem that functions like a BULB.

crown (1) The part of a PERENNIAL plant immediately above ground level. (2) The topmost branches of a tree.

cutting A section of stem, root or leaf encouraged to grow to increase stock.

Above: When you have picked the fruit, cut old leaves off strawberry plants and remove any unwanted runners.

cuttings potting mix An inert growing medium (i.e. containing no plant nutrients) designed to promote the rooting of a CUTTING.

damping off A fungal disease affecting seedlings grown in overcrowded, poorly ventilated conditions.

dibber A small tool used for making planting holes.

farmyard manure The waste of farm animals (vegetarian only) that is incorporated into the soil to improve its structure or spread on the soil surface around plants as a MULCH. Farmyard manure should be used in this way only when it is well rotted; fresh manure can be added to a GARDEN COMPOST heap as an activator.

fertilizer Any product that promotes plant growth.

fleece A lightweight, permeable, usually opaque material, generally synthetic, that is used for tenting plants as protection against frost or spread directly on the ground to warm up the soil.

frame *See* COLD FRAME.

fungicide A chemical preparation that kills fungi. It may be applied either as a liquid (to growing plants) or as a powder (to dormant bulbs).

garden compost Decayed plant remains, stored in heaps or special bins and allowed to break down over a period of six months to a year. Vegetable peelings from the kitchen can also be added, but not cooked foods or dairy products.

grey mould (botrytis) A fungal disease that is prevalent throughout the growing season, especially on plants under glass, encouraged by damp, stagnant conditions and dryness at the roots.

half-hardy Term used to describe a frost-tender plant that can be safely grown in the open garden in summer.

harden off To acclimatize young plants to outdoor conditions by placing them outside in a position sheltered from wind and strong sun and leaving them there for increasingly longer periods. At night, plants should be moved under cover, into either a COLD FRAME or a greenhouse. They can be planted out once all danger of frost has passed.

layering A technique used to increase stocks of shrubs and climbers by pegging flexible stems to the ground.

leaf mould Fallen leaves of deciduous trees and shrubs, collected and stored until they have broken down completely. Weed-free leaf mould makes an excellent addition to POTTING MIX.

mildew A fungal plant disease associated with cold, damp conditions.

mulch A material that is placed on the surface of the soil around plants. Mulches can help to protect plants from frost in winter, keep the soil moist and cool in summer, suppress weeds and (if organic) improve soil structure and feed the plants as they break down.

oxygenating plant An aquatic plant submerged in a pond to increase the amount of oxygen into the water.

perennial A plant that lives for three or more years.

potting mix This term covers a range of soil mixes, some for specific types of plants, used for growing plants in pots; *see also* CUTTINGS POTTING MIX, GARDEN COMPOST, SEED POTTING MIX.

pricking out A technique used for growing on seedlings. Once the seedlings are large enough to handle (holding them by the leaves,

Above: Low-growing herbaceous plants can be kept upright using proprietary support systems. Put these in place early in the year so that the plants grow up neatly through the framework.

not by the stems), they are removed from the trays or pots in which the seed was sown and potted on into larger, deeper pots, in which the spacing between them is increased.

propagator A closed case for germinating seed and growing on young plants. Some propagators contain a heating element.

raised bed A flower or vegetable bed raised above ground level.

rhizome A modified stem that develops at ground level to store energy.

seed potting mix A soil mix that is formulated (usually with low fertility) for germinating seeds.

seedling A young plant that has been raised from seed.

tender A term used to describe a plant that is unable to tolerate freezing temperatures.

thinning Reducing the number of seedlings in a space to prevent overcrowding when seed is sown *in situ* in the garden. Thinned seedlings can either be discarded or planted elsewhere in the garden; in the case of salad crops, they may be eaten.

truss A bunch of flowers or fruit on a single main stem.

tuber An underground storage organ, with a function similar to that of a bulb. Dahlias and begonias grow from tubers.

Index

*Above: The stately
flower spikes of the hardy
perennial* Acanthus mollis
*appear in late summer,
and can be cut and dried
for winter decorations.*